3

One Friday Mom helped them all get in the van.

The Trip
to the
Park

Written by Helen Depree
Illustrated by Bob Kerr

Mom likes working
at the retirement home.
On Fridays,
she takes the elderly people
out in the van.
They like going out in the van
with Mom.

When they were all in the van,
Mom said, "Where do you want
to go today?"

"We want to go to the park," they said.

She took them to the park.
They got out of the van
and walked to the children's playground.
They sat in the sun
and watched the children play
on the swings and slides.
Mom sat in the sun
with them.

Then Mom took Mr. Williams
for a walk.
He wanted to look at
the ducks on the pond.
He wanted to feed
the ducks.

Mom parked Mr. Williams
and his wheelchair on the path
by the pond.
They looked at the ducks
swimming on the pond.

When the ducks saw Mom and Mr. Williams,
they swam to the bank.
"Quack, quack, quack," said the ducks.
They got out of the pond
and waddled up to
Mom and Mr. Williams.

Mr. Williams threw the food
to the ducks,
and they ate it.
Then they quacked for more!
"Quack, quack, quack!" said the ducks.

One duck started fighting
with the other ducks.
One duck ran away
with some of the food.
"You are greedy ducks,"
said Mr. Williams.
"You will have to take turns."

When it was time to go home,
Mom helped Mr. Williams and the others
get into the van.

She drove them back
to the retirement home.
"Thank you for taking us to the park,"
said the people.
"We have had a lovely day."